Melodies of the Heart

SOFT EYES IN THE GARDEN

Bethani Grace

REJOICE
Essential Publishing

Annette Haggett/Rejoice Essential Publishing
PO BOX 512
Effingham, SC 29541
www.republishing.org

Unless otherwise indicated, scripture is taken from the King James Version.

Melodies of the Heart/Bethani Grace

ISBN-13: 978-1-956775-75-4

Contents

Manifested Formula

FULL OF WISDOM, BURSTING at the seams,
hungry children, pure concentrate.
Paying close attention, they watch and await.
In a path that's right, brightness fills the room, with elusive
light,illuminate.
It just radiates, its frequency...the speed of sound,
creating condensation in a glass full of water,
Trickling down the sides and steaming moisture on the walls.
Drip, drip, drip from the faucet nearby,
a stream appears in the room, a river begins to flow in the land.
The sound of rushing water
opens all senses, strengthens every gland,
watching as the message appears, like writing in the sand.
They can just sit here and soar full of life this day,
as the teacher leads the children in deep song.
They know the words
and the beat of his heart.
It makes a wave filling all around,
of knowledge and understanding.
The third button gives way...loosens.
This concludes one lesson,

thus making room for a whole lot more.
And the best is yet to come.

POEM 2

Works for Our Good

YES, WHAT THEY DID wasn't right, but I've got
to forgive and move forward
to embrace the
better in store He has for me.
It's all worked out for my good, you see.
It taught me so many things; the Lord's power was made real
to me.
He lifted me up even when I couldn't see,
and through it all, it brought up the best in me.
It has woven together more wisdom and knowledge,
on a mission to proclaim the good news.
To wake the dead and charge them to new,
with more anointing and even more ammunition than before,
worked out to be a part of God's plan.
My desires are the same, and the dream is alive.
I can see it flash in my eyes, coming closer every day,
because it was His before it was mine.
He has entrusted me
to help others who may have fallen, been broken, or been
abused,

who can't see where they're going or don't know how to get there.
To splash out all that's within me, silver and gold,
I don't have,
but what I have, I give to you.
To sell all that I have to follow the One who has held my life, restored my youth
and everything else back to me.
To give my entire self to be used for the Lord,
who has already given His all for me to be standing here proclaiming the good news.

See, they tried to stop the flow; they tried to stop the dream, but my life was and is in God's
hands. It was His plan for me in motion before I even dreamed it.
That's why it hasn't come unglued
because His plans never fail. His plans are truth.
Now my desire has yet become even stronger,
and I'm going to use it to empower you.
The heart that beats within us and everything else
belongs to God and Him alone.
You can do all things through Christ who strengthens you.
You were wonderfully made—made in His image from His very hands, made a little lower than the angels, and made for His great pleasure.
And He saw that it was good.
When we call on Him, fall onto Him, there's nothing He can't do.
He can raise the dead, and I'm one of them,

a witness, alive to tell about all the great things He can do.
All the great things that He is,
letting Him reign and letting Him flow up and out.
Nowhere I'd rather be, nothing I'd rather do than
to spread His love and His mighty, empowering touch—
a touch like no other, an electric charge that no other surge
could do.
It's true when we give Him our all, He gives meaning to the
abandoned.
His strength is made strong in our weakness.
He goes through every broken place, rips out every tear, and
fills it with His peaceful wine to overflow, molds us to His
likeness.
And we are made whole.

Strength Empowered

YOU PROMISED ME THAT You'll be with me if I
can just see through the
eyes of faith.
I will reap the harvest if I do not grow faint
while You lead me,
because I know that through all of this, You're only trying to
teach me.
I'm just thankful that You won't take Your hand from me,
and I'm thankful that I am not where I used to be,
fighting for my air and my right to breathe.
So someday this, too, shall pass and will also be behind me.
I in You and You in me, I'm walking in victory,
no matter what because You are with me.
I know that I'm getting closer and closer to my God-ordained
destiny, which was written for me even before the hands of
time.
I swear I will make it this time
with no more stagnation and no more defeat.
Your strength is my tower, and Your words, a lamp unto my feet
to walk this path that You are continuing to clear for me.

And all these pains just like the others that have faded into memory but were used for great purpose in which was to lift me up and out.

And the oil used to help others out of their drought,

to rise above it, flying higher, painting flowers on an upright canvas along the way.

With overcoming wind, You fight for me, and I am free today.

So with a new song in my heart and sling in my arm,

as I'm watching You take that rock and thrust it with power,

I know I'm without harm.

Giants fall dead on the ground before me,

just like all the others that are now behind me.

Trust Align

ALL I EVER NEEDED was someone to believe in me,
understand me and take my hand and guide me,
lead me with love and understanding,
with gentleness, inspiring,
and to hear some uplifting empowerment like, "I am proud of you."
After all, how was I supposed to teach what I never even learned,
and how was I supposed to give out what I never got the chance to feel until now?
The rise of true love on my way to being truly free
was how it was first designed to be for me.
See, throughout life, it seemed like I was fighting battles that weren't even mine.
Taking up energy, taking up space in my mind,
had to let it all go.
Shake off the habit of independence
and trust in the unknown.
I had to sell all I had to grab that one thing that was for sure
And hold on to the promise that was ordained divine.
Obeyed instructions in the process and followed the lead.

And had faith that everything was going to work out just fine.
So now all that I am seeing is success that's mine for the taking.
I'm shooting for what is mine from before the hands of time.
Cannot waste any more time chasing after water in deserted lands when now it's raining down reign from the spring inside of me, even strengthening my hands.
And this kind never runs dry.

The Words I Love You

The words I love you never felt so good,
a love so powerfully deep that it can bring tears to your eyes,
something I've never experienced before in my life.
To know that I am loved,
from the inside out,
it just brings me to my knees.
To know that someone is here for me
who would never leave my side,
even when, at times, I've tried to hide.
You gave me space; You just patiently awaited me
till I came around, my feet on the ground.
Hands held out, You've captured my every tear,
fought for me, piercing through every fear.
You took my hand, and we'd gently go
down, down, down,
submerging then pulling on up,
up, up, and out into the flow,
drifting here away with You.
Here I am!

Emerging out of me
in this eternal glow,
my true identity
in these never-ending moments with You!
How comforting to know, comforting to feel
something true and oh so surreal.
In this reality, still waters and free,
while this burning, growing warmth inside
takes ahold of me.
The oil from healed wounds,
filled to the brim of all I've ever craved for.
You've rescued me from death.
I'm alive again,
and now it's the knowing.
With no more lack and thirsting no more
or sharing with others, my cup runneth o'er.
Helping me understand in Your words prevailing,
in this journey of walking home with You.

The Promise Foretold

CHILD, YOU ARE MINE.
Beautiful shall flourish through the rain.
In her, I take delight.
In the garden, she'll remain within fellowship in the day
and a light by night.
Playing music before My throne,
in new songs of praise,
My glory will be engulfed around her.
Precious is the fruit of her womb,
the branches off the vine of the tree, birthing in new elevation
of purity, My covenant for eternity.
For what was once edged in stone is within her heart.
Blessed is she whom I take delight, precious in My sight.
My glory shines forevermore.

POEM 7

The Time Has Come

PACKING BAGS,
    leaving some things behind,
        on my way to my promised land,
heading on out to where I'm supposed to be.
Running full force into destiny,
I don't have any more time to waste
this last time.
Cast my pearls everywhere
for people who didn't even care,
you got too much invested in me
to just sit around and waste it away.
So this time I'm not messing around.
Got things to do like bless this crowd
of people who came from far away,
who truly in their hearts seek you out.
For so long bound in chains and ties,
within "never amount to anything" lies.
Held all the pain behind these eyes
with all my treasures locked deep inside.
Walked around feeling dead alive,
till one day you came and said,

"Girl, come on get out of bed.
The dead will bury the dead.
Come follow me instead.
Got so many things to show,
I made you an igniting light to glow."
So here I am standing here today,
blessing you all with His words to say.

POEM 8

Hands of Time

I'M THANKFUL FOR THE Lord for being my eyes when I couldn't see,
    sending angels to surround me to help and guide me
through this life when I didn't have it all figured out.
Learning to lean on You entirely was the best choice I ever made.
You became real to me and not just a familiar name.
You took me for a walk in the valley fields
and said, "Watch what I can do."
A field of dried-up earth, a field of flowers with no life.
He took my hand and motioned with His hand.
He commanded out His mouth a glorious sound.
As we walked by, a fresh wind began to blow across the land.
One word, one command, and just passing by,
one by one the flowers came to life and all things breathed anew.
Rain began to fall, and their petals gracefully opened,
straight to the core, straight to the main vein.
Opened to the latter rains, dullness splashed with color.
The enemy caught the flame, all his tares ripped out, every stem

mended,

every hair numbered.

For He never sleeps or slumbers,

every wound oiled, restored to better as before.

"Had I said I'd send you to a desolate land and not restore?"

I was taken on a journey through the hands of time.

Picking up the missing pieces, molded, mended, His words came to life.

In the great preparation that will reach the nations of His great love,

who restored all the things that have ever been stolen,

gathered all that have drifted away out to sea,

bringing it close to the heart like a masterpiece.

A treasure held, that'd been yours right from the start.

No more distractions, focused straightforward,

focused straight ahead, where the sun birthed over the horizon,

there was a light for the way.

Dusting your feet from the pain that was never yours to claim.

So as you give it all away, it disintegrates into thin air,

its ashes turning to beauty within the hands of time.

The flowers of the field received their fresh wind,

and one by one they went from trash to treasure.

They all sing out to him a new song, and he hears; a delight to his ears,

and He called every one of them out by name.

Rise and shine, their stems renewed from inside out,

stronger and more vibrant than before.

All lost time recovered, and they were empowered with a brand-new name,

never to be put to shame...ever again.

Spoiled Plot in Victory

THEY TRIED TO WRECK me, but see, they could
not succeed,
because I am Yours and You are mine,
and I was created for Your great pleasure
through these hands of time.
You saved me from the snares of the fowler.
You've tucked me deep inside this heart of mine
that's Yours, always has been
and always will be.
O Lord, I swear I'll get it right this time.
Lead me down this right path that You chose for me
before time began.
I'm going to make my stand and grab hold of all Your promises,
hold them tight what You restored to me
and use them for Your glory.
So much You have for me and for all mankind.
Your love is ever abounding,
so much I can hardly attain,
for all that You have preserved, all that You have

kept and didn't let them take from me.
It was all Yours anyway
right from the very beginning,
and now I'm going to use it, never abuse it,
hide it, or even box it.
I'm giving thanks and praise
for You breathed life into me
and for all to see
what You are to me.
All that You've kept, all that You've done,
the whole time You never left me
but raised me up from low to high.
So thankful for the things I've learned along the way.
You've taught me how to live more abundantly,
a love like no other,
a spark that lit inside me.
Now look, the rising sun
shines bright upon the rock.

POEM 10

Table for Two

SOAKING IN YOUR ULTIMATE light,
in true love's delight.
Your warmth surrounds me,
Your presence here
in this atmosphere.
A table set for two,
for me and You.
You point Your hand above us
to a star lit, and you grab it down,
a harmonic sound,
a beautiful melody.
Your hand held out to me,
like a diamond, all sparkling.
You place it in my hand,
and with Your hand in mine,
You move our hands upon my heart,
a perfect plan right from the start.
A heat vibration illuminates straight through my entire being.
Blessed are Your ears for they hear and Your eyes for they are
seeing.
Like a ripple effect in the water from one drop of rain that fell.

I receive my sight, I open my mouth, and you fill it; I'm alive to
tell of Your good works, of Your awesome wonder,
of Your knowledge, and of Your splendor.
A treasure gained, Your glory known,
I am Your beloved, the apple of Your eye.
Nothing can harm me, for I will live and not die.
You never left or forsake me.
I in You and You in me, I am free!
Filling me with Your wonder, filling me with Your words,
filling me with motion,
filling me with Your love,
filling me with power,
You are with me wherever I go.
A dove appears and flaps its wings in our midst,
and a feather falls,
mine to keep, I grab ahold.
A pause in time,
the river runs up my spine.
The most beautiful sight I've ever known,
out my mouth in overflow.
I seek and find a release of life,
the release of purpose unfolds.

POEM 11

Free to Shine

MY DREAMS, THEY ARE still alive.
Had to let some things fall from me,
that didn't mean me any good,
that only held me down.
Had to change my mindset,
change from defeat to a victorious state of mind.
Had to let some people go
to release the negative
and allow the positive to continue to grow,
to surround myself
in whole new surroundings.
Being introduced to greatness,
a new part of life
that I've never known was intended for me.
An experience like never before,
a rising up from the inside out,
feeding my true potential.
A flourishing garden like the garden of Eden,
attached to the vine and a well that never runs dry.
Tares taken out,
the old left behind.

Found treasure that I'll never let go.
True love cherished
beyond the human mind.
Acceptance without rejection; inside shining.
No longer having to fight
chase, prove, or find.
It's here; I have it
flowing like a river
inside of me.
No longer running in place,
no more sinking sand,
but on solid ground I stand.
I am free.
Found out who I truly am,
in a place where I belong.
Slave clothes taken off
and received a brand-new garment.
In my rightful place,
holding onto what's rightfully mine
with a glow upon my face,
free to shine.

POEM 12

Overflow

PRECIOUS LAMB OF GOD,
that blood that was shed so unselfishly
for me so that I could live and not die
and stay the apple of Your eye.
That blood that washed me white as snow,
in experience Your glory known,
in the love that You have shown.
Kept me safe in your hands,
and against all odds, I came out alive
but purified.
You came in and dined here with me,
never left my side,
in a peaceful, harmonic glow from the inside out.
Oh, my God, my heart changes beat in great thankfulness.
When I think of it,
it's deeply rooted, and the garden continues to grow,
filled with new wine,
in constant overflow.

Take a Walk with Me

TAKE A WALK WITH Me.
I can show you things,
 secret things that are revealed within My eye.
Things that you know not,
treasures of inheritance,
that only within Me you can find.
I am the door,
I am yours, and You are Mine.
A covenant.
Pure intimacy.
All My words they come to life
before your very eyes.
Deeper understanding
carved in the inside,
My temple,
My dwelling place...
Wisdom beyond recognition,
wonders
that your eyes have been given to see,
and your ears they are Mine to hear.
Intelligence like none other,

there is none besides Me.
Child, you are Mine.
You are a part of Me,
chosen before time of excellence and creativity.
My plans and purposes unfolding,
led deep into the promised land.
Being a part of the movement of My hand,
you're presented as a woven masterpiece.
Greater works than these
for all to come to see
and know Me personally.

Breakthrough in Knowing

BREAKING THROUGH THE AIRWAYS,
breaking through membranes of resistance,
pushing through the walls of any muscular limitations,
looking past the spectators from your past,
the walls fall down.
In confidence and in boldness,
you're given a new gown,
not allowing your greatness
to be hidden on some shelf.
Someone may need to hear what you've got to lay down,
what you must speak about.
Your work is never done in vain.
It's all part of the journey,
it's all part of the gain
of all giants slain,
coming out in victory
and setting others free.
In being the blessing,

rising above all expectations
even your own.
Letting God have complete control
so you know you're good to go
to the table prepared for you
in celebration.
Giving God the glory,
this is where He saw you before you were even born.
You've made it, you've won it,
and He's so proud of you.
Only the best for you like every parent wants
is right here in store for you.
There's such a great reward
in giving it all you got.
When God is for you,
there's nothing in the world
that can be against you.
Just give yourself completely,
and in all things be glad.
Be careful not to become upset.
If results had taken longer
or even shifted in a different route
than you had originally planned,
our thoughts are not His thoughts
and things will go exactly how they should.
You do your part, and God will do the rest.
It's all birthed in perfect timing,
and remember, where you are now
isn't even compared to where you're going.

Here with You, Here with Me

THERE'S NO PLACE I'D rather be than here with
you, here with me
and the places you take me when I'm lost in these
moments with you.
There's hardly the words to describe your hold on me
and how much you mean to me, if I could just spill it all out in
how much I love you.
Like a waterfall that feeds into a never-ending river that flows
throughout the land,
I'll never thirst again.
If I could just record as a movie these visions within my mind
in you,
to share these amazing glares for you,
swept within a whole other realm inside these eyes with you.
Such a sweet surrender, this heart melts as one with you
in your awesome splendor.
Your glory comes down, and the earth shakes like thunder.
The eagle takes flight and scans the earth below,

like a watchman with its God-given keen eyesight...oh, how beautiful the views.

The wind, it blows freely, sweeping across the land.

The birds whistle their songs of praise; the scent of flowers ignites the air,

especially after the rains. The sun, it appears above the horizon as it paints its golden shimmering light like a blanket of diamonds within the sand.

Standing here with me, lost in this moment with you...

There's just no comparison anywhere

than being here with you, here with me,

lost in these moments with you...

The Proposal of Purpose

HAVE YOU HEARD THAT you couldn't do it
and that you wouldn't amount to anything?
Do you know whose you are
and how you've come this far?
By whose hands you've been created and your purpose in this
place?
Do you feel Me tugging?
Do you feel Me speaking?
You know who you are when you are alone and undisturbed.
In your eyes, you see yourself there,
to a place that I have designed just for you.
Allow Me to come in and make all things new,
to get you to that place you dream about,
to that place that's only for you.
It's waiting, the true you
that you know on the inside of you,
without weights and without boundaries,
without tears and without heartache.
I'm waiting for you to hold out your hand.

Take Mine, and I will show you.
I will lead you there from the inside first
to fill you with My life,
the life intended for you.
Will you trust Me?
Give yourself completely to Me?

The Making Hands

FROM THE MORNING SUN,
when I rise to seek Your face,
and throughout my day a continued thanks and praise.
Your words, not mine,
Your plans succeed and prevail my life.
Even at night to the setting down,
when I take my rest,
Your angels surround
and Your glory manifests.
Determined to give my all to You
'cause You're the only one who can bring me through
to the other side of the expected plan.
You've proposed for my life from You.
Nothing can hide from You.
Everything that stirs inside,
mending and molding of perfection and gold.
Everything that I am, everything that I have, You hold.
To everything, there is a reason, and to everything, there is a season.
There's nothing too little or too few.

There's nothing too hard for You.
There's nothing that was made without a purpose.
From the bottom to the top, a seed in the ground
grows to the surface.
Everything is Yours.
Nothing can stop Your creation
with Your hands in affiliation.
To Your name always be glorified,
Your name always be magnified.

The Healer

I WILL HEAL YOUR BRUISED muscles,
fill your wounds with oil,
and bring forth rain in the dry places,
flood it out like a mighty flowing river.
For I have heard your prayer supplications before Me,
both silent and spoken.
The swollen membranes of tension suddenly will become relaxed and open,
for you will take part in it no more.
The pain and aches of yesterday
will only be that of a memory,
of lessons learned and triumphs earned
from this day forward.
For you have not given up hope in Me
and cried out continually.
Great strength is now your portion
and freedom your reward,
for I have watched and see you grow
from putting away useless complaining
and held tight to the promises of My word.
You grasped ahold of its concepts and looked past the seen,

and that was faith in the making.
I've watched you grow from independent thinking
to relying and leaning on Me completely,
because you knew you couldn't do this on your own.
That has stretched you into a beautiful mold.

POEM 19

Shelter of Refuge

HE SEES YOUR TEARS, and they are many,
even the ones you do not let roll down your face
for anyone to see.
The ones you hold deep in your heart are the ones that need to be released.
You don't have to prove anything to anyone.
It's wasted energy; we grow tired, and we try to get there on our own, with all the opposing people and opposing winds.
That's why the Lord is our strength, our shield, and we hide in the shadow of His wings.
Let God mold you into the place you're trying to get to.
Don't go ahead and try to get there too fast
without proper positioning.
It just won't last.
Trust in the Lord's perfect timing.
By letting go and letting God, you will see you surface automatically, fully, wholly, and completely.
Even the environment will shift as well
one step at a time.
Prince of Peace, Lion of Judah,
trust and have patience in His perfect timing.

The Finished Piece

HAD TO FINISH UP some final touches
to show you what living life truly means.
The giving up oneself and all foolish lies
and in-betweens that once plagued your mind
and blocked your dreams.
Put your complete trust in Me,
acknowledging you couldn't do this on your own.
Giving up independence, working with your own strength,
and finding Mine,
it works every time.
The places I can take you
have, and continuing, are far greater
than the things you've left behind,
restored to even greater.
Now I've prepared a table
filled with a special anointing
that can only have been given within time.
Look how My glory shines.
I am alive,
gleaming with pure light
that cuts through darkness and brings to life

the very works within Me.
The creation of My hands,
I take delight.

POEM 21

Heart's Melody

AS SHE SITS AND writes,
a supernatural paintbrush
and sprinkles of oil upon her hands...
A heartbeat,
a music melody
pouring out
what's inside me.
Breeze in her hair,
my presence everywhere.
A willing vessel.
Articulate sounds of heaven
and the abundance of rain,
splashes of color,
work never done in vain.
The fire of my touch
and the growth and life within my flame.
Health and healing,
the deliverance of the captives
birthed anew and set free.
Unlimited access to my glory and my reign.

Timetable

THE PATH AND STRUGGLES that you walked through
and overcame all led you to this point of prosperity
and a compassionate burning flame
flickering inside you
in purpose unfolded.
The time that I spent there,
as I observed in the spirit,
the inner child and I took a walk
down memory lane.
I was brought into recognition,
the realization of where I've been in life,
all the things that I've ever been through,
where I am now,
and where I'm heading to.
It was made perfectly clear to me
where the Lord was bringing me,
the generation before and after me,
up and out of,
and to God be all the glory.
So when I walked out that door,

there went the past stripped and shed away from me
and the new in a never-ending pour.
I gave the old away,
and some was stripped because it could not stay.
I laid it all there at the feet of Jesus.
I had stepped into a new life
and to live it more abundantly,
the life that was tended and meant for me,
subscribed and written out for me so perfectly.
The whole land was healed on that day
when I let go and gave it all away,
the inheritance of new land promised to me,
even that promised land from those before me.

Bought with a Price

WHEN I THINK OF all that transpired in my life
and all that You have brought me through
and all that You show me even now
and how Your word had become truly written in my heart,
through it all I experienced Your deep compassion for me,
in deeper understanding,
and understand clearly that Your word sent forth I can stand on
and that Your angels hearken unto Your word, and they really
do stand by our side,
encamped around us.
When I think of how much I grew through it all
and how I am here still standing
because I fully relied on You.
You took me out of that pit and really breathed life into me,
not just physically but spiritually too.
You have all things under control, and we learn to completely

let go and let You do Your will.
When we completely look to You for all things,
that's when we find out that we don't have to carry anything.
You bring us through.

That's what Your word is sent forth to do, Lord.
When I think of who You are
and all that I have learned
and how You brought me this far,
a tear escapes my eye.
I couldn't have made it without You,
and all I can say is, oh, my God, I thank You,
for You truly did have me in the palm of Your hands.
As my heart beats, it will forever beat.
I thank You, thank You, thank You, Jesus, thank You.

The River Inside

FOR YOU KNEW ME before I was born,
   as a child, I remember singing songs of praise to
   You,
that even my toys would play concerts to You.
But somewhere along the way,
I lost my thoughts and lost sight of You.
And just like what You said in the garden,
"Where did you go from me?"
Somewhere in this life, the wolf came in,
tore me up, spit me out,
and left me for dead therein.
But You heard my cry and my plea
and breathed life into me.
With an anointing that breaks yokes of bondages,
You took me up, and we went for a walk into recovery.
You unveiled the mystery.
You slowed me down and opened my eyes so that I can see
and allowed me to keep the plans You set out for me.
You didn't let my enemies' triumph over me.
Instead You had a table prepared for me.
You swooped and covered me

so that no harm could come to me,
gave to me real life
and to have it more abundantly.
You took out the junk that they left behind
and filled me with love, life, and prosperity.
Now this river inside wants to give You glory,
and Your heart, O God, pours out of me
Your love so intensely.

A Rising Symphony

HEADING STRAIGHT TO YOU
and all You have for me,
that's the only answer I'll keep.
Your gleam in my eye and the trophy within my reach,
You've shown me so many things already,
and still the better is arriving.
Accomplishments unthinkable,
it feels so good to finally achieve
and live within my purpose and my dreams,
Your plans from the very beginning.
You're the truth and the life.
I'm getting it right this time
with Your help and to God be all the glory.
Look how He illuminates even the thoughts I'm writing,
how He took me from one place to another,
from the pit of failure and defeat
to a palace of my heart's desire that He had first already given
to me.
A seed is planted inside of me.
I took His hand, and look where it brought me—
Success and victory,

Unlimited possibilities,
My dreams coming true,
Dignity regained,
cracked open and renewed.
This is who I am,
blooming prosperity.

Mind Renewal

CHANNEL YOUR THOUGHTS
in a rightful manner,
giving all our worries and pain
into the Lord's hands.
Breathe out the old
and breathe in the new.
Never allow anyone who looks down on you
to plague your mind.
Forgive them quickly and get rid of it
and know that you are wonderfully and fiercely made.
Bring out that passionate fuel within yourself.
Keep your head up,
keep on smiling,
and keep on moving.
Let your love for people and life
outweigh and overshadow
the false views about you.
Never let their doubts stop or hinder you.
Soon all will sit down and continue to watch you glow
and see that you were, indeed,
created to shine.

Keep going forth
in love and prosperity.

Sparked Ignition

EXPECTATIONS ARE THE GUIDE,
faith alive, supernatural experiences bursting from
the inside.
The forces and manifestation collide,
springing forth fountains of life from within.
Dancing in vibrational waves of His glory,
in a detailed glimpse of a relational story.
The mist of heaven fills the air,
His presence fills the atmosphere.
The Lord be magnified, His angels on standby,
He brings health to our bodies and deliverance to our soul.
A beam of light stems from the throne,
through us His glory shown.
Being receptive to His heartbeat,
nothing compares to the heat of His awesome wonder
and the power in His voice like that of thunder.
The heavens declare His declaration,
and it spreads to all the nations.
Every tongue, every tribe,
His awesome greatness abides.
To him who believes,

calling Him forth,
inviting Him in.
Everything that He created
is put into a proper place,
for His word prevails,
sent forth and reaps a harvest.
His purpose unveiled
through picture, a vision,
through dream, a mission.
Signs and wonders, they follow,
led by His Spirit.
We give Him songs of praise,
heavenly music, what an awesome sound.
His glow on our face and His glory in His place.

Flight Aglow

IT'S TIME TO SOAR like an eagle.
It's your time to shine
that ever-elusive glow.
It's time to reach out and grab it.
It's all in my hands.
All of it's mine.
And to you it's been given
since before time.
You've made it.
You've come along.
You didn't give up.
And now it's time to show
the world just how much you really know,
to show what you're made of
more than you have ever seen,
more than you have ever known.
Flying free like an eagle,
accomplished long-awaited goals.
Such a great feeling,
blessing in the development.
All your time and all you've sown

was completely worth it
in how much you've grown.
A treasured masterpiece
in the hands of the Creator
the entire time.
Nothing could harm me
because it had to go through you first.
Thank God you knew my heart
and my intentions
to someday be used
to help save the world.
Into your hands this day
and every day, you bring
such a beautiful amazement
to your wonders unscathed.
Enlightened and strengthened,
smooth sailing from here on out,
such a huge advancement
overtook the land
in which you gave to me.

POEM 29

Your Time to Rise

THE WAIT IS OVER.
They are no longer sitting in the shelf.
They are in my hands,
and I'm handing them out one by one.
I'm here to say that
no matter what you may be going through,
there's a time for everything,
and it will pass through.
You will get to the other side
and feel anew.
When He wraps you in His arms,
there's nothing He can't do.
He will take you there.
Just wait and see.
The view from the after is worth the going through.
Pain won't last forever.
Through the process,
you'll see what you've been called and made to do.
One foot in front of the other,
that's all you have to do.
Grab hold of the One

who got the strength to pull you through.
Paying close attention to all there is to learn,
you'll see in the end
that you came out not even burned.
You came out even stronger,
blessed, and highly favored.
Through it all,
there's a lot to be thankful for.
Just hold on tight,
grab His hand,
and you will find
just how He pulled you up and out of even yourself.
His glory shines through,
making you into the you
you always dreamed of,
with more knowledge
and the glow of the sun.
Every hair on your head is numbered.
You were made an overcomer.
You were made to pull through.
Go on and grab the prize.
Cease the moment.
It's your time to rise.

You Are My Covering

YOU ARE MY COVERING.
Now I know the intensity
of the reason why You bled and died for me.
So You could conquer that grave
and free my way ahead of me,
before the path that I'd take.
You knew me and already planned an escape.
You loved me that much.
To lay down Your life
in such an unselfish sacrifice
so I could live and not die.
A love that great,
nothing could ever compete.
And now You are here with me,
Your living Spirit inside of me.
You walk with me,
talk and guide me
here into eternity,
in a duet,
a precious melody,
in perfect harmony.

When You move, I move.
When You rest, I rest.
I don't ever want to step outside of that.
You are my protection,
and just like a parent,
You say things for good reason.
It's for my own good.
I thank You for watching over me
and having Your angels take charge of me.
Staying within this dwelling,
no harm can ever come to me.
I call on You in everything I do
and wait for You
to guide me into what to do.
You know all and see all.
You are my covering.

Wings like Eagles

Mount up with wings like eagles.
Imagine flying above the clouds
in a serene place not far from here,
with a view of the river and land down below.
A beautiful, soft breeze,
a constant flow,
the scent of flowers illuminate your senses,
filling your heart with warmth enrichment.
The mountain view is incredible
as the view of your newfound home comes into sight,
a city on a hill, full of delight.
The land is just flourishing.
Liquid gold, manna increases,
overflowing, new, and improved.
Open land and freely you,
even beyond what the eyes can see.
So much room to move around,
move around indeed.
Your gift, it makes room.
There's nothing you can't do,
filled with endless possibilities

in the land of plenty, a garden abloom.
Guarded on every side,
angels surround and in Him abide.
A peace that surpasses all understanding,
provided for, cared for in divine protection.
He gives you power to gain wealth,
the wealth of the wicked laid up for the just.
Visual insights and vivid sounds,
an endless stream forever flows.
Destiny bound, an ignited burst, a sudden thrust!
A fresh wind sparks your spirit inside.
Welcome home.
I'm alive because He kept me.
Right by my side, He never leaves me.
And all this land promised
is given to me.

My Alibi

M Y BEST FRIEND,
my alibi
watched over me.
Blessed to know you
since the day that
you walked into my life.
Greatest work accomplished
from one seed sown.
My alibi,
such a beautiful melody
beats from this heart
to overflow.
So thankful a feeling
to know you are not alone.
My alibi,
a love I carry with me
every day and all day long,
moments to cherish.
A captured song
when written together, it can't go wrong
My alibi,

you took my hand and led me,
walked with me and helped me grow.
You mended my wing, and on that day that I should go,
a tear escaped from your eye.
As I take flight, from your hands, you have known.
My alibi,
you are forever a part of me
and forever for you a place in my heart.
Many can come, but none can compare
or take the place of the special bond that we share.
And it is a song just for you.
My alibi,
I will always remember you,
near or far or wherever you may be.
There's no time in between.
You're always here with me.
My best friend for eternity
and all that you are to me,
my alibi.

Beautiful the Horizon

BEAUTIFUL THE HORIZON
as they sat on the deck, reading
and spending time with God.
Quietly listening for a whispering, leading
the start of prayers throughout the day without ceasing.
Catching a glimpse in vision of what's being laid in their heart
while witnessing the rich gold beams of light.
Paint crimson the scene as the sunrise
rises in its strength and canvases the skies,
warming the earth and all that abides
as it climbs above the trees, illuminating their eyes.
Look how the sun shines and beautifies the horizon
when its warmth touches even the depths of your soul,
knowing the Creator is with us wherever we go.
The birds also sing their praises, welcoming the morning.
The music of the heaven's realm, the sound radiating the earth
in dance as they capture this all in a visual freelance.
His presence all around, it sets off a beautiful fragrance,
embracing the moment that marks the rest of the day,
a reflection of love in a never-ending duo lights the way.
And what a beautiful breeze that blows across their face.

A sensual touch is captured in which to trace,
a sparking in their heart and its flowing richness in their hair,
the refreshing scent of the warming morning dew fills the air.
Enlightened with peace and rest,
the glory of the Lord at its best.
His creation is beautiful inside and out,
when we take a moment and notice the work of His hands
that fills the whole earth and blankets the land.
It's great to be among the land of the living,
to receive from the One what's been freely given.
Even with Him, a relation
in a solitude dialogue,
to open and receive the greatest of love.
A fellowship spreading to the whole nation,
filling Him with great joy and pleasure.
A love that is without measure,
for He is our portion, a lasting of forever
that nothing can ever sever.
Taking time in giving thanks for life,
the gift to see, to hear, and the reception to feel.
The love of the Creator who has it all
and yet takes the time to be with us all,
to embrace His touch, to see His beauty.

Chain Breaker

FOR BEHOLD, I STAND in the heavens
with the sword in My hands,
ready to strike the atmosphere
with the powerful weight of the promises
I have for you that fill the heavens.
With one strike, it will shift the whole, entire universe
and atmosphere in a ripple of effect that is so big,
held up from before time began for you,
to show My glory through you.
One strike and My power will come upon you
so strong that whole nations will feel the wave of My glory.
Many lives will be touched by My Spirit through you.
Behold, I am ready to pour out the heaviness of My blessings to
you to feed a whole multitude.
One strike and the heavens and world will shake and tremble.
For what I'm about to do for you and through you
will start a whole revival of atmospheric surrender,
a healing and deliverance, for many will see
and come to Me and be set free from all bondages
and sicknesses in transverse

all within one wave of My glory.
In your songs of praise, I will enter the place,
and all will fall to their knees in awesome wonder
and feel the heat of My presence.
A community chain breaker,
a breaker indeed,
not by might or by power
but by My Spirit.

Fall like Rain

THE BLESSINGS JUST CONTINUE to fall like rain
and your sunrays upon my face.
The heavens open, and the earth shifts,
your presence in this place.
A prayer with you face-to-face,
like fire in my body.
A candle burning within me ever abounding
sweeps me off my feet.
The warmth of the flickering flame of a love astounding
captures my heart like no one else can.
A song fills my heart,
and it whirls within me and then goes before you.
I can't help myself; it's so overwhelming.
Of all the things you are to me,
of how much you mean to me, it comes out,
so much for me to attain.
My cup runs over and pours out unto you like an aroma,
and suddenly, a sweet wooded fragrance,
a mist fills the room, the scent of your embrace.
You are welcomed here, I need you,
and I got to have you; nothing else will do.

Nowhere else have I ever felt this feeling.
Nowhere else have I ever seen such beauty,
like the rising of the sun in its continuity,
a river flowing in this land with its sound of life,
and the sound of the wind gently blowing.
You are speaking, your countenance flowing.
I take a breath, and I breathe you in; you are with me.
The scenes open before me,
a visual showing.
I draw you in, and you draw to me.
You show me things that no man can
and teach me in greater understanding.
No good thing will you withhold from me.
What is for me is for me and no man can take.
I speak, and you hear me.
I'm tuned in to you, in love with you.
Lowly and meek, your heart I seek and I find.
The door opened; I am enlightened.
A wisdom and knowledge
obtained that one cannot gain from college.
A peace, a calming, a release, a lifting,
so fulfilling in its place,
so unique, mine to keep.

I Need to Hear You

I NEED TO HEAR YOU.
I need to hear Your voice,
to know what You have for me
so it would be without void
and be filled with Your glory,
secured and filled with Your love.
I need to hear You.
I need to hear Your voice
in what You have planned for me
so I don't go my own way, by my own choice,
or my own words.
I don't want to do anything
or go anywhere
if You're not there,
that's for sure.
I need to hear You.
I need to hear Your voice.
Speak Your will for me.
Speak Your will into me for my life.
It's Yours, not mine.
So I may glorify You and bring You joy,

be a blessing and bring light to the night.
I need to hear You.
I need to hear Your voice,
for what a beautiful sound in my ears
and a comforting flame in my heart,
knowing You are here and You'll never leave me
and to know for sure where You send me.
You'll be playing Your part, which is without fail.
To do my best and to give my best,
and You, faithful and true, will do the rest.
You are in control, not me, not anymore.
Block anything that's not in Your eyes
for me, for You,
for the people that You'd reach for You.
I need to hear You.
I need to hear Your voice.
Fix my ears and cradle me in Your arms.
Clear the way in the path before me,
lit up and obvious, because You'll be here with me.
Your thoughts on me more than the stars
a reflection back to You
for who You are
flowing through me.

Living Inside

AM THANKFUL TO BE alive and granted to be
among the land of the
living
so I can go on carrying out what my hearts been driven
to do for You,
and to You more will be given.
Sooner I tried,
but I could not see it clearly
until You...
And now I see it all worked out perfectly,
right now and right on time.
With more to pour out
than what meets the eye,
more than I ever thought possible,
until You came and changed my mind.
To him who has, more will be given,
with more to contribute
and even more to find,
right within arm's reach
and even inside.
I've made it this time.

So thankful to be in the right mind.
All that searching,
all that once pausing,
what seemed like blind
and going nowhere.
All that scattered
had come together
in an organized manner,
focused and determined,
moving forward.
Now I'm somewhere
even the gates of hell cannot prevail against
what God has ordained
and what God has blessed.
Now the knowing,
showing, and glowing,
flowing to the outside,
I found it, my place in life.

His Word Comes to Life

YOU LEARN THE WORD of God from a whole new prospective.

His word takes on a whole new meaning; they become real, written in your heart,

health and healing to your bones,

a cleanse to your mind and bandage for your wounds,

a protection like no other.

Keeping our eyes on the Lord and looking straightforward,

it opens passages you didn't even expect in favor like never before.

If you don't quit and keep speaking and proclaiming His word,

you'll see them at work for you, maybe not how you intended it.

We make plans, but the Lord orders our steps—His will, not ours.

Things will work out for our good, and His words, you will see come to pass

in exactly what was designed for you when you recite them into the air and wait on the Lord to carry it through.

He stands by His word and performs it.
You begin to see His word with a new pair of eyes.
Deeply rooted, it comes to life.
You learn what it really means to have God on your side.
His word is the light to your path and a hammer to shatter,
a fire to burn and water to quench,
a sword to slice and strength for power,
a guide for truth and a guard to protect.
Nothing is impossible.
The Alpha and the Omega, the beginning and the end,
who created everything and whose hands can do anything,
His words really do make an impact.
And time spent with Him, drawing near to Him and He to you,
dwelling in the secret place,
there's no better place for you, such a great peace within,
not as the world gives but for yours to win
and to spread the good news of His huge love for me and for
you.
And if you give it a shot, it's not really that bad to submit to Him
'cause there you'll find that everything you ever needed
was already there and yours to have.
He knew us before we were even born.
See in the world we had become bound,
but in Him, we are found again.

Love Is Here to Stay

LOVE WAS BORN, AND love will burn forever.
Hate could not put out the flame.
It may have broken a bit throughout life,
but I have recovered and have been reborn.
I have returned to my original form, from before the world began,
to carry out my mission even more
and with more to give than before.
One thing was for sure, love could never be suffocated,
renamed, or even put to shame.
Love can never die inside, and for the rest of my life,
it will remain alive—birthed and first given.
From above where it was first known, tapped inside and flowing from home,
and to God be all the glory, a rainbow shines so beautiful in this story.
Love inside will continue to fly; it cannot be hidden or disaster-stricken.
That was the plan of the enemy, but it was nullified.
See, even attempted to destroy the temple, but it was rebuilt in three days.

Even the love from above could not be choked.

So how did they think my love inside would die?

If at first from above it was given and to the one who has risen.

I was tainted for a while, yet my love remains alive

and even rising up with more strength this time.

Can you see the flower as it grows from that seed?

In your eyes' vision, as this, you read.

And how does it rise up with strength in its stem?

Then blooming in the suns delight,

Almost suddenly, instantly in a quick-moving film.

How does it move from day to night?

Once I learned who I am, and who I am is who I am supposed to be and that nothing was ever really wrong with me.

It was just a lie that was forced for me to think, but now it's gone,

and I am like a tree,

making an impact on those all around me.

Love was created to live; it can't be kicked around,

left to die, or even forbidden to live.

See, I'm rising up inside; all glory to the One who created me this way.

A Place That's Known

OH, WHERE ONE CAN go if allowed the mind to just soar,
open the heart to a whole new world,
an opened door.
Together we can go for a walk and just explore
endless possibilities in life's creation.
All that one can imagine, oh, but so much more.
A butterfly on the tip of your finger,
like a child free at last, free to dance...
In a place full of wonder
within reach, one can behold.
As one dances, gracefully smiling and at peace,
a knitted garment of flannel and of fleece.
Bare feet in a field of flowers and a river that flows around,
you can hear the beautiful sound of its run,
a run that never dries and is never undone,
not even from the heat of the sun.
A pasture, a meadow, and a swing for fun,
outlining trees for shade and for shadow,

a painted canvas of beauty and tranquility.
In your mind, a peaceful flow
that never grows old and can never be sold
but merely given, free as you know.
In sight and in vision,
the scent of life all around,
is yours to cherish and yours to behold.
Glitters of life and of gold
float freely like lightning bugs
and feathers that fall and tickle your nose,
full of laughter and of love.
Holy Spirit fire and a dove,
lilacs and cedarwood,
and the wind, it blows as it should.
Nothing to abstract, distract, or hinder you.
Free in flight.
Come and go.
Stay or take it with.
It's yours to have, yours to hold.
Forever,
the covenant it speaks,
within view a golden city
feels like home.
Infinite watches over you like a dome...

The Bow of Victory

HE DROVE OUT MY enemies one by one
until not one was left standing.
He kept me and preserved me
and taught me wisdom along the way.
Now I have all the bows and arrows in my hand
from all who oppressed me.
With the Lords help and leading,
I've taken possession of the land.
There is none other like the Lord,
who upheld me in His hands
and set me among the people.
Though I didn't understand
His plan at first,
it has taken away my hunger
and quenched my thirst.
The plan unraveled before me as I went along.
He showed me His power,
He showed me His love,
He showed me His might,
that I just cannot get enough of.
He rules, He reigns

in everything He has made,
and the work is never done in vain.
He set me apart.
He has set me free.
Now to show the world
His redemption, I sing.
There is an end to suffering.
I hold within me His promises forever,
to pour out a story,
one after the other,
of His grace and glory.
And never have I ever
seen the righteous forsaken.
The tools of the enemy
has been severed and taken.

Silence Is Broken

IT WAS ABOUT BEING content within yourself,
knowing to be patient in growth,
understanding that growth takes time.
The knowing not to rush ahead of God ever,
not expecting anyone to do it for you
but understanding you couldn't do it on your own.
Raise your self-esteem.
What you have to say matters.
Just because people are watching
doesn't always mean they are waiting to mock or laugh at you.
Forgive the past and let it go.
Speak anyway.
Just let it flow.
It was a deep-down embedded fear that you didn't even realize
the reason for your silence.
The silence is broken,
and fear is shattered.
It's time to rise up and speak no matter who's around.
Picture the crowd as they speak in different tongues.
Eventually, before your eyes, what you have to speak will be
spoken.

The whole crowd will be in tears and be set free from oppression,
depression.
Hindrances will blast to pieces.
Hearts will be cleaned,
cleared, purified, and healed,
set free and delivered.
Don't doubt yourself and your abilities.
I AM needs you,
and so do the millions of others who are waiting on what I've
prepared you to do.
It's in your belly; it is coming out of your heart,
waiting to be poured out.
The foundation has been set.
You're coming out, and your out is setting the captives free,
like Moses getting the children of Israel out of Egypt.

The Spring Fountain

HE TAUGHT ME HOW to fly high
above the clouds,
above the noise,
and above the sounds.
He taught me how to live life
more abundantly,
more fluently.
His majesty, it overflows
into my life,
living through me,
healing all my wounds,
bringing me to life from the inside,
showing me and guiding me the way to go,
how to be loved, and how it truly feels
to be protected and to be loved truthfully,
to allow love in and finally able to embrace it
and let it all in without fear.
He showed me who I truly am
by taking away all the things that caused me harm,
even removed the plague that for so long captured my own
thinking,

pulling up and out of me, the me He first created me to be.
Filling the empty with what I was always seeking for,
I got it right here, Him with me through this open door.
I am wonderfully and fiercely made in His own image.
In time spent alone with Him, a journey to heaven here on earth,
manifesting my life in rebirth.
From bottom to top, walking with me into prosperity,
a gem, a diamond, a ruby,
a masterpiece in the making.
A flower that He calls His own,
He taught me how and without feeling guilty
to love myself in His love filled to the brim,
splashing and outpouring.

Determination

LORD, I CAN'T DENY Your presence here with me
    when the blessings just fall like rain
    and even in my dreams.
You're my portion; I am complete,
and it's great to know that You are here with me.
You never leave my side,
even when at times it felt like You were so far away.
And it took all I had to press forward
and press into the beam
of Your everlasting, loving, ever-forgiving, graceful light.
When the things in this life tried to hold me down,
through all their dragging and pulling at me,
I still reached out my hand
because I knew that wasn't the end,
and through it all, I knew You had a great plan.
I kept on pushing, kept on pressing in,
kept on seeking Your face.
I knew you weren't far.
I've always been in the palm of Your hand.
You were always within speaking distance.
You're my best friend.

So I gave it all I had,
wasn't going to give up,
determined to make it.
Perplexed and shaken,
but not dead,
my inheritance was to live.
For You I had to keep up the fight
because I knew You'd make it right,
and when I became exhausted,
you were right there with a fresh wind,
to fill me up,
to take off the weight,
taking my hand and growing me up.
You showed me Your flame.
You caught them on fire
and breathed strength into me
to get up and move again,
even when at times I couldn't see it then.
You were always right here with me.
It's evidently clear, and through it all,
it's become even more real to me.

Grand Opening

CAUSE I WANT TO give You my all, oh, give You my all,
give my all to You, Lord.
There's no more time to waste,
can't keep just sitting here,
so let's spill Your heart out into the atmosphere.
Come now, Holy Spirit,
Your grand opening,
for all to see and hear the songs You sing to me,
a wave of sound
into the air around.
I'm coming into destiny
in doing what I was created to be
before they tried to rob from me.
I'm going back into the hands of time,
so take my hand.
Grab what's mine.
Now come and dance with me.
You made it, you see,
in victory.
To God be all the glory.

We made history.
I'm walking in it now for what You gave to me
and to use it for Your glory.

Place of Security

IN THIS PLACE OF security,
there's no place I'd rather be.
Better is this place of rest I find in You
than a thousand elsewhere.
A moment of escape with You,
strength renewed.
My life is not my own,
and through it all, I'm thankful for what I've been through.
Through it all, You've never left my side.
To lack from the world is to gain
the true fulfillment of what life truly means,
a true appreciation.
I'm so glad for it all
because I know where the true stem of love comes from
and the only true place to find it and never lose it.
I'm so glad You drew me close to You
even from before time began,
so I wouldn't have been "lost in the crowd."
I'm so glad You called me by my name.
"Child, You are mine."
I am the apple of Your eye,

and nothing can separate me from Your love, God.
Things fade, but You remain.
Your love endures forever, and it goes deep.
There's no place I'd rather be
than in this place of security.

A Basket to the Children

DON'T DO IT BECAUSE I told you so,
but do it to save your own soul
and to save others whom you may not even know,
for what I say and pour out,
it comes from my heart,
and I really mean it.
Our decisions and the words we speak
can mean life or death and all the time in between
for this generation into the next
and for those who aren't even here yet.
For the things of this world may pass away,
so we save ourselves treasures that remain forever,
and the day will come when you'll remember the words I have been
given.
You'll remember the words; they have been spoken.
That you'll see with your own eyes
and your ears will hear it clearly
and your heart will receive its elusive memory

so vividly.

So take these words and hold them close.

Eat of this wisdom when you're walking down the road.

Promise me this, that you'll never turn from these words I speak to

you

so when adversity may come to try to steer you toward lies,

you'll already be prepared, and you can walk away

just from the words I speak this day.

Don't let them bring you down.

Child, stand your ground.

Keep your eyes on the light and let God show the way.

He'll never steer you wrong.

His glory is such an awesome song.

So go on and win the prize that is edged for you and you alone.

Finish the race of time and space

in straight-up victory

for all to see

the glory of our King,

and always let your faith abound.

Because I hear the sound

of abundant rain,

know that your work

is never done in vain.

I'll Love You Forever

'LL LOVE YOU FOREVER,
and there's so many reasons why.
You were my eyes when I could not see.
You gave up Yourself so unselfishly.
You weren't afraid to take that plunge
to leave the ninety-nine
just to go after one
and spent Your time with me
while I was in recovery.
When I was poor, You clothed me.
When I was hungry, You fed me.
When I was thirsty, You gave me a drink.
When I was sick, You sat by my side.
When I was in prison, You visited me.
You stood and watched over me entirely,
the willing vessel to help breathe life back into me.
You took the time to sow into my life,
for You knew it was worth it, and You thanked God for it.
Others walked away,
scattered even from the weight of that adversity
that wasn't even mine,

that was given falsely
and was sent out to kill me.
But I cried out, and the Lord heard me.
He sent me the best warrior for the job.
He sent me You, and You didn't flee from me.
You stayed and prayed with me,
spread the love of God through me,
opened my eyes in a whole new level entirely.
I experienced His healing fire through my bones,
and it shot straight to my soul.
Picked me up and gave me hope,
see what You've done for the least of these?
Now I pray the harvest; You enjoy the feast.

Touch the Hearts of Many

YOU WILL TOUCH THE hearts of many,
and even the hardest of hearts will feel the light
of the spark of My words in your mouth.
Their pains will be released to the heavens above,
giving them hope and endless love.
The seeds planted and sown
will prosper new beginnings,
awakening each flower to grow
to a flourishing, vibrant garden, all aglow,
birthing a new generation of celebration.
A renewed symphony in the air,
bringing dry bones to life,
breaking and shattering strongholds,
I will be there.
This is My better in store for you
before you even got here.
I was there and here
as a journey unfolds
that only you've been birthed to hold,

for the least of these.

Hope

HOPE,
the unfailing response from within,
a locking grasp of strength and ability
to look beyond the natural and win.
Holding onto the trust that the train driven by God
will take you to what He has shown,
designed and ordained for you to hold.
It's never giving up,
breathing in and awaiting in expectation,
with patience and serenity.
It's the undoubted fragrance of tranquility.
You watch as your dreams approach within your reach.
Glistening warmth succumbs you.
A smile graces your face
as you look toward the east,
as the sun just peaks over the horizon.
A melody plays over and over deep within your heart,
a deep connection from heaven above.
The ever-elusive precept and acknowledgment
that this has been "meant to be" since before time began.
A fervent love inside that can never cease,

a graceful dance in the garden,
depicted and known.
The growing flight of the rose
in the garden of treasures unfold.
That's yours to keep, an eternity threshold.
Destiny revealed. Hallelujah forevermore.

True Love

TRUE LOVE FOREVERMORE,
for I came down from the secret dwelling place
and became your friend.
I walked and experienced life with you,
got to know you.
My love for you is so deep
I sacrificed Myself for you.
Even though I cried out to God to take this cup from me,
in obedience, I still carried out Our Father's will.
I was sent to pay the price for My friends
and laid down My life for you.
I was beaten and bruised
so I could take the "pain" from you.
Three days later, I rose up from the dead and ascended into
heaven.
Though My body is gone,
My Spirit still lives.
And I will always and forever be here for you.
I laid My life down for you,
even if you chose not to live for Me.
I accepted you, even if you do not accept Me.

I love you and always will,
even if you don't love Me.
My love is unconditional.
I am true love.
For I am He who is speaking to you.

Eternal Flame

A CANDLE LIT, A TREASURE gained,
the flame softly flickers before me.
"The Melody of My Heart"
is a prayer laid before you.
You quiet my soul.
I relax in your warm embrace.
Everything around me disappears.
Breathe out the old, breathe in the new.
With my strength renewed,
my spirit lightens; the flame inside
begins to "soar" freely.
An angel dances gracefully,
moving to the "winds" of your voice,
of one mind, of one accord
in deep connection.
You are the flame that burns within me.
When the Spirit moves, the flame moves.
When the Spirit is still, the flame is still.
Eternal one! Consuming fire,
consume me.
You are the light, the very life that burns within me.

Without you, my life would burn no more.
You, oh guiding light, are the one
who ignited my dreaming splendor.
My trust, faith, and hope are in you.
This is my heart.
So my candle, it burns
and can never be put out
because its anointing fire
is from you.

Praise Him

PRAISE HIM LIKE YOU got it
'cause it's already been done,
doesn't matter if you can't see it.
Girl, you'll surely see it, and you'll surely see it, son.
So keep your head held up and don't look down
'cause you don't want to miss it
while messing around.
Praise Him in advance.
Praise Him with the dance.
Hold your hand out, ready to grab it,
'cause it's falling down.
The wind is surely coming fast.
Don't want it to pass,
pass you by
while focusing on the waiting
and not the receiving.
It's a celebration in your heart like the Fourth of July.
You'll receive it if you don't deny.
He can do the unthinkable.
He can do the impossible.
No battle too big and no battle too small

for the Lord God Almighty,
who already gave His all.

In Time of Escape

THROUGH THE WILLOWS AND the whispering winds,
sitting near the riverbed, skipping rocks on the water,
spending time with you,
to just allow of my heart to cry out,
to replenish, refresh, strengthen, and renew.
I call forth the heavens, fall down on me.
Having, at times, these burdens that touch my heart,
some not even my own that weigh and pull at me,
that circle the unknown.
Having so much to say, and speaking, but seems sometimes no one hears a sound.
I watch as people pass by as if I'm not even there.
He speaks, but is it heard?
Does it fill anyone with hope?
I speak this sincerity to you,
having a passion for mankind...
A need to reach the people to spread love,
kindness, a word of knowledge, and even a spoken direction,
tapping in because your strength pulls me through.

Sometimes it seems there is no one around,

no matter even within amid a crowd.

But You, O God, are there, hearing every word,

every whisper, and familiar with every need,

speaking and sensing Your words that never touch the ground

but paint a picture of life surround.

To feel Your touch, to feel Your presence burning and splashing

life back into me,

filling me to the brim and running over, a peace like no other.

A moment of release,

a relief that no one else can give.

These pictures in my mind, a whole movie.

My purpose is pulling at me, so, Lord, I ask that You take these

words that I speak to You.

You know my heart and everything that it needs, for it beats

for You.

So take these words that I speak

and give them away to touch them,

pouring and blessing with them to whom You please.

New Life Rising

PUSH PAST THE PAIN of ridicule and shame.
Push past the discomfort and let go all the pain.
Push past all the disappointments.
Trust God in every moment and all circumstances.
Believe it's possible that your situation isn't too impossible
for God to change and rearrange,
for He created all the heavens and all the earth,
the oceans, the valley, the clouds, and the rains.
For everything, there is a purpose; for every reason, there is birth.
Believe you are not counted out but set aside for something great.
The next generation to make the earth shake.
Push past all doubt
and command the limbs to sprout.
New life and strength that's sparking flame from deep inside
and clinging to the promise and proclaiming,
"What's mine is mine.
They're not taking it from me, no, not this time.
And this is not the end. I'm climbing, and I'm rising."
Determined, strong-willed, and priming,

drinking from the wine
and feeding from the vine.
Grab the hand of the Creator,
lifting up and out from the depths of your soul.
Walk on solid ground
and continue to prosper,
no longer on sinking sand.
For the very hairs of your head are numbered,
each and every one,
not by might or by power
but by His Spirit.
The Lord is for me; He's created me
for this very purpose.
He has preserved me.
So my heart's desire
can still be a blessing.
The I AM within me
knocked out every single opposing thing,
gave me knowledge, wisdom, and breath to sing.
So every dart and every wrong
turned into even deeper compassion,
victory rising strong
in "to God be all Glory" songs.

I Love You

I LOVE YOU,
and I really truly mean it.
I thank You for waking up all my God-given senses
and not letting them defeat it.
Instead You increased me
and used it for Your glory.
I thank You for preserving me.
I thank you for keeping me.
I thank You that I am able
to still write my story.
With every gift
and with every talent
that's all from You anyway,
it wasn't wasted or thrown away.
I thank You for trusting me
And filling me with Your glory.
Let Your name be magnified.
I just want to bless You fully
With every breath I take.
With every breath I take, Lord,
I love You.

Bless Your Holy name.
Have Your way.
Your way is just.
Your way is good.
Your way is prosperity.
From under the hood,
in every single way,
in every single day,
I love You.
You can never fail.
Nothing comes back to You void.
It accomplishes everything You say it will,
including me.
With Your plans, I succeed.
I thank You.
I love You.

Thank God for Everything

CHERISH MOMENTS THAT WILL last forever,
and forget moments that have no rights to your happiness.
Appreciate what you have, never taking anything for granted,
and what you're not a part of anymore,
let it go so you can grow.
Call out the things that will be.
Write them out plain as can be.
Claiming them already there
and, one moment at a time, you'll see
all things are being organized,
set up,
placed,
coming together perfectly.
Journal your growth.
What a success.
What a story.
Give God the glory.
What a blessing.

Strengthened and free.
Live, love, laugh.
Be thankful you're not where you used to be.
Thank Him for where you're going
With sincere certainty,
thank Him right where you are at
with every breath.
Fellowship to behold
and moments to remember.
And one thing we ask
is to remain in the house of the Lord forever.
Thank God for everything.

Transformation, New Sight

GO FROM FIGURING EVERYTHING out on your own,
having all the answers,
to having to completely lean on God and trust in Him
to work out everything
and do what no man can do.
Things that were unseen by man was seen by God.
Nothing is hidden from Him
So it was a step into the unknowing
and trusting in God to pull off the impossible.
That was a big change,
a huge transformation.
That was growth from the inside out.
That was watching a miracle take place and be in the middle of it.
That was walking in the realm of the supernatural
and grabbing keys to new ground you didn't think you had access to before,
watching the supernatural unravel before your very eyes.

Inside your own body,
inside your own mind,
like snowflakes that start to fall from the sky
when there didn't seem to be a cloud in sight,
so suddenly, so naturally.
That was the Lord showing Himself strong in your life,
knowing Him on a whole new and different level,
him showing you that He has everything under control
and that you didn't miss your flight,
opening your eyes in a whole new sight.
Like laying down your life and watching and witnessing the
Lord pick it up again
and restore it like nothing ever went wrong,
surpassing all calamity into all things made beyond right,
right where they should be.
Still you, but in new sight.
Surfaced anointing.

You Can Have What Is Written

HE HEARD MY EVERY word,
saw every tear,
felt every pain.
He gave me back what they've tried to take from me.
He destroyed all the lies that were ever told to me.
He ripped me out of the prison they laid for me
and took out the poison that they planted into me,
purified my blood,
purified my heart,
purified my spirit,
and redeemed my soul from their grip.
He gave me back the life He planned for me,
even more than I had even dreamed.
He stood for me when no one else did.
He believed in me when no one else did.
He loves me in a way that no one else can.
When all hope was gone and man could not help me,
He listened, heard, and rescued me,
touched the very depths of my heart.

I will never be the same.

He gave me a second chance to live and didn't allow them to take from me

or continue to take from me.

In fact, He turned it all around as if what happened never even existed.

He healed, delivered, and strengthened me.

He became truly known to me.

I honor and cherish Him.

When I had no one to turn to and all my trust from mankind was gone,

He helped me believe and trust again.

He made me brand-new again.

He freed me beyond freedom in the human eye.

I am forever thankful and will speak of His good works

and spread His love and His power like wildfire

because that is what He gave to me to do.

He is my shepherd; I shall not want.

He is beyond reality, all I ever need.

His presence here with me,

a relationship with me,

He brought me up and literally made me whole.

Complete Restoration

LORD, EVEN WHEN IT seems
no one else could possibly understand,
I know You do.
Before I can even speak a word,
You see all things,
all the tears, and all that happened.
You know it wasn't the ending.
I'm just getting started,
and I know You wouldn't allow
that which You ordained for me
to be taken away,
hidden, buried, or barren.
So I believe,
believe with my whole being
that You are with me.
The whole earth can pass away,
but You remain the same.
Lord, even when it seems
no one else is around,

Your presence is what I seek
because I know in Your presence,
demons tremble
and the whole earth shakes.
The trumpet sounds,
and Your glory
lights up the place.
My skin is renewed,
and the youth returns to my face.
My hair glimmers with new life,
flowing as if no one ever tried to kill it.
And I believe You can pull off the impossible.
My bones extra rich in marrow,
my life restored back to before they tried to take it.
So my gifts and my calling,
my all, wholeheartedly
multiplied, amplified,
to give You glory
in this story
of how, O Lord,
in complete restoration.

On Everything in View

LET THE GLORY OF the Lord fall down.
Let the glory of the Lord fall down.
Let it fall like rain
unto this place
and unto this place.
He shines His face
on me, on you,
on everything in view.
Forever here with me,
the anointing of
His presence, two become one, intimacy.
His glory forever,
And it's only begun.
His awesome wonder.
There is no other,
no sensation,
or any other thing
that can even compare
or can ever take His place.

Not a thousand people
or any living thing
can give me what He can give me,
a satisfaction guaranteed.
Miracles take place
when You enter my space,
acknowledging You in every and all ways.
The garment of praise,
A light that shines our way.
Let the movement of His mighty hands
take us straight through,
straight on through
to the promised land
of His heartbeat,
in the palm of His hands.
Let the glory of the Lord fall down.
Let the glory of the Lord fall down.
Let it fall like rain
unto this place
and unto this place.
He shines His face
on me, on you,
on everything in view.

The Faith Watch

DOESN'T MATTER IF YOU don't think it can be accomplished in time.

God knows it can and will; just have faith in Him.
Take Him at His word, make that first step, and He will do the
rest and shoot you the very best
that He has in store for you.
He will blow your natural mind.
Watch, He will do it, you'll see,
shorten the amount of time it would normally take
to get it done and, for His name's sake,
quicker than if you tried it on your own.
For it's supernatural,
and with God, all things are possible.
He can do anything.
Watch how,
if you give Him your all,
watch how it flies.
Completely rely,
do not waver,
and trust in Him
and believe!

Recite His words back to Him
with faith that moves Him,
even as small as a mustard seed.
How His words can move mountains,
blow up barricades,
and even breathe life into the dead.
How He blesses the fish and the bread
and feeds the multitude,
turns nothing into something and parts the Red Sea...
How He can speed things up,
multiply it "on the dime,"
and fall everything all into align
all at the perfect time.
So watch and do it His way, you'll see,
and what's best for you
will come to pass easily.

The Finding in Recovery

FOR YOU DID NOT wish for me
to live in pain and misery.
In the pit, they secretly laid for me,
but You brought me out
and fed me through that drought
and broke off the chains
of shackles and pain.
This work was never done in vain
Oh, how You must have cried through a thousand rivers of tears
as You watched me be misled, used,
then abandoned and abused.
Oh, how I rushed and went ahead of You,
went in a way of my own leading
instead of Yours.
Though my intentions were well,
I landed myself in the middle of a war zone.
But I looked past the warning You gave,
and that almost put me in the grave.
I never knew people could be that cruel

without a care in the world,
a part of life I had never known.
But You, O Lord, were still there
to pick me up.
All I had to do was call Your name,
and You heard my cry and my plea.
You came to my aid with mercy and grace.
You were right there to rescue me
And turned it all around for my good.
Now I'm still able to carry out what was meant for me to do.
Some intense learning came about in that season of my life.
I came to know You on a deeper level,
and I never denied it
but found out how real You really are.
I experienced it personally,
the warmth of Your healing,
the love of your touch,
the power of forgiving,
and the strength of Your delivering power.
You didn't leave me there like that.
You picked me up, and we had a deeper chat.
Your words came to life before me.
How precious Your anointing.
Now words are written in my heart.
I couldn't have made that out alone.
I'm thankful for You.
Oh, how I need You and Your guidance every second of my life.

Anchored

THE LORD GOES BEFORE me.
The atmosphere shifts in my favor.
His favor is like a shield.
This is the day He has made.
I rejoice, and I'm glad in it.
A light like a fire around me,
His glory surrounds me.
He is with me wherever I go.
A wind blowing,
His kingdom come,
His will be done
on earth as it is in heaven.
Strength.
A team of angels,
they hearken unto His word.
I am anchored in certainty,
greatness, and truth.
I am blessed and highly favored.
He gets all the glory.
And I anticipate the good news.
He never upholds anything good from me.

Everything good comes from the Lord,
the creator of the heavens and the earth.
And the fullness thereof,
I was created for His great pleasure,
and with His righteous hands, He upholds me.
Great plans He has as He leads and guides.
He is right there in front as He touches...
a glimmering gold,
setting everything into place as we go.
Integrity, confidence, and bold.
Everything I touch prospers.
I open my mouth, and He fills it.
Wherever my feet tread,
what is for me is for me,
and what is given to me, I behold.

Protected Destiny

I MAY HAVE BENDED, BUT I did not break; now
the mountains to move
and the earth to shake,
miracles manifest in Your presence no doubt.
Debts cancelled, sicknesses removed.
Deliverance, greater works than these.
Beyond expectations, hearts atoned.
You meet everyone's need, for You have held me, preserved me,
guided and taught me newfound wisdom that's mine to speak
and to share to those who seek.
You have entrusted me in this land that You gave to me.
The transferred wealth, a treasure box of hidden riches,
You gave me the power to gain wealth,
not just with my hands but within my soul,
rising like the sun in its strength.
You met me at the well.
You have taken the keys of death from me,
kept me from harm, and allowed me to see
and witness these things.
You took a walk with me, and within it,

You have and continue to bless me.
Who am I that You'd be mindful of me
and blessing others as I go?
It cannot be stopped, limited, or restricted.
Oil to be poured out,
Your power is shown.
Your grace and Your mercy
and Your love are never-ending.
All things work out for the good,
the righteous never forsaken.
As Your purpose and plan unfolds,
written before I was born,
giving water to dry land,
food to the desolate,
security for the searching,
and strength for the broken,
my mission, Your promise
is chosen for purpose.
Unscathed and unharmed,
and all for Your glory.
I searched, and You gave to me.
I knocked, and I have received.
You've uncovered the mystery and, within it all,
moments of deeper intimacy.
Through the fire, but not one hair was burned
because You were with me,
a protected destiny.
With every arrow, a double blessing.
The anointing, blinded eyes opened,
scales removed, breeches restored,

and a heart renewed—Your word a whole new meaning.
A deeper relationship with You!
A greater understanding
in deeper truth and revelation.
Alive to be poured out to all mankind.
Unraveled before my eyes,
Your words in my mouth and deeply woven in my heart.
Your words like honey, nourishing and flourishing faith abloom,
a tree with deep root expanding and branching out,
speaking truth.
Your kingdom come, Your will be done.
Your purpose and plans prevail.

A Fragrance Unique

THE BLESSINGS JUST CONTINUE to fall like rain,
And your sun rays shine upon my face.
The heavens open and the earth shifts,
your presence in this place.
A prayer with you face to face.
Like fire in my body, a candle burning within me ever abounding.
Sweeps me off my feet.
The warmth of the flickering flame of a love astounding.
Captures my heart like no one else can.
A song fills my heart, it whirls within me and then goes before
you...
I can't help myself it's so overwhelming.
Of all the things you are to me,
of how much you mean to me,
it comes out, so much for me to attain,
my cup runs over and pours out unto you like an aroma,
and suddenly a sweet wooded fragrance...
A mist fills the room, the scent of your embrace.
You are welcomed here, I need you, got to have you, nothing
else will do.
Nowhere else have I ever felt this feeling.

Nowhere have I ever seen such beauty.
Like the rising of the sun in its continuity.
A river flowing in this land with its sound of life,
and the sound of the wind gently blowing.
You are speaking, your countenance flowing.
I take a breath and I breathe you in, you are with me.
The scenes open up before me.
A visual showing. I draw you in and you draw to me.
You show me things that no man can and teach me in greater
understanding.
No good thing are you withholding from me,
what is for me is for me and no man can take.
I speak and you hear me. I'm tuned into you. In love with you.
Lowly and meek, your heart I seek, and find.
The door opened, I am enlightened.
A wisdom and knowledge obtained that one cannot gain from
college.
A peace, a calming, a release, a lifting....
So, fulfilling in its place....
so unique, mine to keep
and to share to the sheep
and to God be all the glory.

Conquered the Unknown

GREAT IS THE PATH You have chosen for me.
I take delight in it.
Your word is like a river that flows
deep within me.
I cling to Your every promise,
for You hide me in Your shadows.
In Your hands, You hold me,
keeping watch night and day,
guiding me through the process.
You give and take away.
You give what is good for me
and take away what's not.
Sleep never enters Your eye.
Your strength, it covers me.
I trust in Your will.
You pray over me
and care for me.
You breathed life into my bones
as I enter and reach toward my destiny,

as the doors open before me.
You never withhold anything good from me
or allowed me to waste my purpose.
In Your freedom
has reached its point of day.
My walls You have strengthened.
You have made a pathway.
I have escaped disaster
from those who sought my life,
and I owe it all to You.
I am alive to testify.
Your power is clearly shown.
For You have conquered the unknown.

Moments Spent with You

MOMENTS SPENT WITH YOU,
I cherish the moments spent with you.
I hold close the passion,
kindling like a fire within me for you.
You send a spark like the shimmering warmth of the sun,
shining beams of light within my heart.
Like a well-watered garden,
you bring the best out in me.
Blanketed in warm conversation,
I come to life and am free,
fully myself with you.
I could remain in these moments forever.
Your love just radiates within me,
like oil in my soul.
Even your unspoken words,
they speak a thousand vibrations
into existence
within the beating of our hearts.
An intimate flame in warm candlelight,

a love felt so deep,
I can give myself away
in these moments spent with you.
It just pours out like a river.
Everything around me just pauses
as I fly away into forever with you.
You draw me close and cover me.
A connected embrace,
a sensual glaze,
infused and one with you.
We drift and dance under the moonlight.
You lift me up, spread my wings to full flight.
An explosion of strength, the height and the length.
Two hearts combined together.
I can stay here with you forever
in these precious moments I treasure,
these moments spent with you.

To Lay Down Is to Pick Up

I ESCAPED IN YOU,
You in me.
You heard me.
You changed my surroundings,
and I gained some clarity.
You designed for me beauty
from the inside, pouring out of me.
And no matter what it looked like,
You were working behind the scenes.
You touched my skin
and kissed my face.
Now Your glory is doubled in this place.
You changed my life
with just one word...
"Child, follow Me,
and you'll be cured.
The only thing I ask of you
is to lay down what is hurting you
so I can take you to that place

that I've ordained for you.
I'll take that thing and turn it around
and turn it into a beautiful sound."
Lord, give me the strength to carry it out.
I trust You to take this desert and take this drought.
Give me water like a spring-filled fountain,
fill me with Your love,
and renew my youth.
Lord, I know You will make it right
because this isn't even my fight.
They hated You before they hated me,
but because You are on my side.
I in You and You in me,
my faith and Your power collide.
I walk in victory.
You are my hearing, and You are my sight.
I trust in You and Your plans for me.
I know You won't let the sun go down on me
because I was purposed for greater works than these
to set others free.
So I trust in You that
You will guide me
and carry me.
I can count on You to uphold me
and give me the strength
to pour out what You have placed inside of me
to be a blessing to many.

Miraculous Protection

LORD, COVER US SO that our minds, hearts, bod-
ies, thoughts, and
actions line up
and remain lined up in You.
You are our strength in our weakness.
We are perfected in you.
Your words bring health and healing to our hearts,
our bones rich in marrow.
You also watch over Your word to perform it,
miracles, signs, and wonders follow.
Your angels hearken unto Your word
and listen for Your command
to surround us and keep us safe.
Your presence is with us, and for that, I am thankful.
We move when You move
and are still when You are still.
For it is in You we truly live,
Breathe, and walk in victory.
You teach us Your ways, for they are best.

There's nothing You can't do.
We believe that all things are possible through You.
It's our faith that moves You.
When our praises go up, Your glory comes down.
Fill us till our cups run over.
Fill this place with Your presence because
being in Your presence fills us with joy.
All knees bow and tongues confess.
Darkness flees, and sickness is swallowed
evaporated, and dried up at the root.
Your fire consumes it and makes us whole,
from the inside out, in Jesus's name.
You are mighty and strong,
and we are your children.
We are redeemed, sanctified, justified, and vindicated.
Oh, my LORD, I thank You!

Flow Dance

LORD, I THANK YOU for the music
that twirls my soul into dancing,
bringing me into a moment with You.
There is no other that makes me feel the way You do.
Makes me want to stay here forever,
eat from the pastures and drink from Your waters.
You are my shepherd I shall never lack.
Your glory fills me, makes me light up and stay lifted in spirit.
I love where You take me.
I love the places we go, and I don't ever have to leave home.
This is where You find it.
Knock and the door is open.
Seek and you will find.
Such an awesome place here inside
and the outside streaming forward,
in the current of living water
and in the garden where the plants meet the sower.
Glory to Your awesome splendor,
so majestic in wonder and power,
such a sweet aroma that fills the air,
Your presence everywhere.

Dancing on top of the water,
with a bright anchored light, I surrender.

Prayer from Within

FOR YOU HAVE GIVEN me a dream for me to
truly live,
it must be carried out.
For if my eyes see it
and in my spirit it is very much alive,
then it is mine and is for certain that it will prosper into reality.
As long as I continue to hold Your hand to where You will take
me,
therefore no limitations or restrictions shall ever hinder me.
Whether it be natural, physical, or spiritual, it shall not stand.
I have purpose.
For You have given me gifts and talents that are being used to
the extreme,
living in a whole new dimension.
That need to be nurtured,
strengthened, maintained, developed, and brought to its fullest
potential is through the roof with success beyond expectations,
even of myself.
And it's mind-blowing.
Your glory falls down, miracle manifestations,
and it's mine for the taking and to You be all the glory.

Because You are my portion and I will not settle for less.

No eye has seen, nor ear has heard.

Continue to sharpen my eyes so that I may continue to see
in full detail and in great understanding.

My heart ever so receptive to Your leading and direction.

Your will be done on earth as it is in heaven.

For what is best for me in my life,

guiding me to Your plans for me and all for You, to give You glory.

Let Your glory continue to fall on me, in me, out of me, and all around me,

Your presence ever abounding.

I trust in You because You do not fail.

I thank You because it's already done, in Jesus's name. Amen.

I Am Speaking

FOR I AM READY to do things for you that you
know not of.

Until you let go of those things that hold you, in-
hibit you,
and keep you standing still, then you cannot fully grasp
the things I am about to do for you.
It's all waiting on you.
See, the enemy tries to retain you where you are,
making you believe
that things aren't going to change,
that you'll just be giving up all the securities
that once worked for you.
All you've ever known that satisfied you
to give it all up in vain
and that you'd be walking out on the limb, blindfolded.
But see, that's a lie.
Even he knows what you are capable of,
and that's why he's trying so hard to stop you.
You need to push at this time.
Give it all you've got
to grab all I have

in store for you,
more than you could ever imagine.
All that's waiting for you on the other side,
what I want to do for you and through you.
It is going to blow your mind and everyone else's.
You know what I'm talking about.
You were born to breathe life into people, naturally,
and you cannot do it sitting on the sidelines.
That is the gift I have given you.
Now it's time to shine.
Your words are powerful,
your heart is giving,
and my anointing upon you will cause many hearts
to catch fire and prosper health in their bodies.
Just by simply hearing and reading these lines,
you have heard me speak to you numerous times.
So it's time to stand; it's time to shine.
Watch for my leading,
the doors I am opening.
Hold onto my staff and part the water.
Watch and see what I am going to do.
You'll be growing and birthing.
You are a firsthand witness
of my power.

Through It All

FOR YOU, O LORD, I must succeed.
There's no more wasting time for me.
It's a must for me.
I want to be ready.
Be in the right moment,
at the right place,
at just the right time.
You see, it's a must for me,
an opportunity of a lifetime.
For You and Your glory shine,
there's a craving, O Lord,
deep inside.
I must put everything else aside.
It all couldn't satisfy me,
deliver, love, or heal me.
None of it could ever take me
where You can take me,
which is right where I need and want to be.
It could never grab my attention and keep it
the way You have laid it all down for me.
There's a need to bless You, Lord.

In a way, how can I ever repay You
for how You have blessed me?
You laid down Your life for me.
Mine is Yours for the taking.
You changed my name,
how You brought me through
from then until now.
Now I sing aloud,
show the world
how through it all,
in gladness and in suffering,
You've been right there with me,
through my ups and downs,
the whole, entire time.
Through it all, You have kept me.
Through it all, You have held me.
And through it all,
You knew what You were doing.
All I needed to do was let You do all the walking.
Through it all,
You continue to shine,
kept the candle burning inside.
You recovered, restored, replenished,
rebuilt, and multiplied me.
You were the strength in my weakness,
Lord God.
You are magnified
through it all.

For the Least of These

I'LL LOVE YOU FOREVER,
and there's so many reasons why
you were my eyes when I could not see
you gave of yourself so unselfishly
you weren't afraid to take that plunge.
To leave the ninety-nine,
just to go after that one
and spent your time with me.
While I was in recovery,
when I was poor you clothed me,
When I was hungry you fed me,
when I was thirsty you gave me drink.
When I was sick you sat by my side,
when I was in prison you visited me.
You stood and watched over me entirely.
You were the willing vessel to help breathe life back into me.
You took the time to sow into my life...
For you knew it's worth and you thanked God for it.
When others walked away

from the weight of that adversity
that wasn't even mine,
it was given falsely
that was sent out to kill me...
but I cried out and the Lord heard me.
He sent me the best warrior for the job.
He sent me you, and you didn't flee from me
you stayed and prayed with me
spread the love of God through me
opened my eyes in a whole new level entirely
I experienced His healing fire through my bones
and it shot straight to my soul
picked me up and gave me hope.
See what you've done for the least of these?
Now I pray the harvest; you enjoy the feast.

To Hear Your Voice

I NEED TO HEAR YOU,
to hear your voice.
in what you have for me.
So, it will be without void
and filled with your glory.
Secured and filled with Your love.
I need to hear you.
I need to hear your voice,
in what You have planned for me.
So, I don't go my own way, by my own choice
or my own words...
I don't want to do anything
or go anywhere,
if you're not there with me.
I need to hear you,
I need to hear your voice.
Speak your will for me.
Speak your will into my life.
It's yours and not my own.
So, I may glorify you, and bring you joy.
Be a blessing and bring light to the night.

I need to hear you.
I need to hear your voice.
For what a beautiful sound in my ears,
and a comforting flame in my heart.
Knowing you are here and will never leave me,
and to know for sure wherever you send me
you'll be playing your part without fail.
I'll work to do my best and to give my best
and you, faithful and true, will do the rest.
You are in control, not me, not anymore.
Block anything that's not in Your will for me,
for your kingdom.
For the people that need to hear you,
need to hear your voice.
Fix my ears and cradle me in your arms.
Clear the way, for the path before me,
will be lit up and obvious because you'll be here with me.
Your thoughts on me more than the stars.
A reflection back to you.
For who you are.
Flowing through me.

Transparent Glass

SHOWING YOU ALL THE things you need to know,
Right up front, right in the flow.
Enlightening all things,
even the things that you desire to know.
For I am the eye,
I am the door.
Take my hand,
walk with me.
Documenting a fine-tuned discovery,
we will travel the lands and explore.
All things opened up, set up before you,
deeper understanding like never before.
The sun and the moon
and everything in between.
The deepest of the oceans,
all that's seen and unseen.
And the flowers richly in bloom,
the light and its meaning that engulfs the room.
Grab a paper and a pen to keep on hand,
like supply and demand.
Keep it near your side and even your nightstand.

Watch the glory, an unfolded story.

Now let's begin.

Feel the raindrops,

and listen to the wind.

Freedoms Redemption

HE DROVE OUT ENEMIES one by one
Until not one left standing
He kept me and preserved me
And taught me along the way
Now I have all the bows and arrows in my hand
From all who oppressed me
With the Lords help and leading
I took over the land and possessed it
There is none other like the Lord
Who upheld me in His hands
And set me like a "king" among the people
Though I didn't understand His plan at first
It unraveled before me as I went along
He shown me His power,
He shown me His love,
He shown me His might
That I cannot get enough of
He rules, He reigns
In everything-He has made

He set me a part, He has set me free-
Now to show the world His redemption
That I hold within me, to pour out His story
His promises forever
Of His grace and His glory
Never have I ever seen
The righteous forsaken
The tools of the enemy
Has been severed and taken

Like a Mist

LIKE A TREE PLANTED, our roots run deep
There, rivers in abundance flow free
Angelic company all around
A beautiful melody, such a harmonic sound
A sense of peace, a fresh flowing breeze
One sits near a waterfall
Where healing waters flow from the birth of the mountain
And from the depths of the earth; a spring fed fountain
With every strum of the harp they play
Golden speckles caught up in shimmering display
Within the sun rays
Shining down from the heavens above
The Holy Spirit, Lord; like a dove
Soaking in Your presence, a place like no other
What God put together let no man put asunder,
A thick cloud from a mountain-like mist
Spreading all across the land,
Your love and Your thoughts on us are greater than the sand.
Hear my cry, oh Lord, Hear my plea
Touch every person; including me!
Everywhere and every place

Pour out Your Spirit, pour out Your grace
Like a mist that went up from the earth
And like, how over the waters-You hovered,
Let not one thing or anyone be left uncovered
By You A protection shield around us like a globe
For You are strong and mighty in whom I trust and put my hope
Nothing is hidden from You
I call forth Angels on assignment to defeat and pursue
Squish this thing like only You can do!
Manifest Your greatness, manifest Your power!
Blessings fall like rain in a supernatural shower!
Make Yourself known
For earth is Your footstool and Heaven is Your throne
Calling down fire from heaven to burn the alters and dry up the trenches
Even the ones that sit on the side lines and all them benches!
There is nothing that You cannot do
Every virus, every sickness, every foreign thing too
Burns with fire like a meteor when it touches the earth's atmosphere
Disintegrates at once, a burst into combustion and suddenly, instantly, it just disappears!

About the Author

ANNETTE HAGGETT IS A prophetic writer who enjoys writing from her heart in descriptive detail. She decided to capture all these visuals and share them with others in this incredible, dynamic book, Melodies of the Heart. Her pen name is Bethani Grace

She was born in a small town in Upstate New York, where she often enjoyed the outdoors in extreme adventures and sometimes getting lost in the field across from her home with her childhood cat. Along with her love for nature, she also enjoyed drawing, writing, and painting. She loved creating. She also starred in her church youth group plays on stage, which would later become a huge part of her passion in life.

As she grew older, she was either acting, teaching in her makeshift classroom, writing stories, or capturing her visuals in a drawing. She was capable of filling a whole notebook with a story in one day, just writing down the visuals that would play like a movie in her head. She is naturally the type that if the crowd were to be turning left she would turn right on purpose. A good part of her life she tried to fit in but never found peace with that until she realized the significance of her indifference was a brilliant plan right from the start. Though she was familiar with the word of God from attending church as a child growing up, she never truly experienced the deep revelation of His word.

One summer, in particular, she had the urge to just read the bible from beginning to end under her favorite tree. After some months of reading, suddenly something just sparked within her and all of her talents and gifts that she had as a child enhanced immensely.

In addition to her writing books, she also is Co-founder of Word to Life Ministries, where she also co-stars alongside her husband on their YouTube channel. Where she infiltrates all her life experiences with the word of God in the pursuance of her being a blessing to others. Her deep desire to project a teachable light onto the course of understanding and obtaining perspective of their own life's purpose and gain momentum in embracing their own unique God given abilities! That of course, can trickle further and burst forth like rushing water in a chain reaction!

www.ingramcontent.com/pod-product-compliance
Lightning Source LLC
Chambersburg PA
CBHW071402120626

46546CB00002B/783